ANIMALS EVERYWHERE
Animal Habitats Around the World

Written by Mia Cassany
Illustrated by Nathalie Ouederni
Translation from Spanish by Little Gestalten

Typefaces: Gotham by Jonathan Hoefler and
Tobias Frere-Jones, Coluna by Marco Ugolini
Printed by Agpograf, Barcelona, Spain
Made in Europe

Published by Little Gestalten, Berlin, 2024
ISBN 978-3-96704-774-5

The Spanish original edition, Animals Mapamundi,
was published by Mosquito Books Barcelona
© Mosquito Books Barcelona, 2024
© Texts Mia Cassany, 2024
© Illustrations Nathalie Ouederni, 2024
© For the English edition Little Gestalten,
an imprint of Die Gestalten Verlag GmbH & Co. KG, Berlin, 2024

For more information, and to order books, please visit gestalten.com/collections/little-gestalten

Bibliographic information published by the Deutsche Nationalbibliothek.
The Deutsche Nationalbibliothek lists this publication in the Deutsche Nationalbibliografie;
detailed bibliographic data are available online at dnb.de.

This book was printed on paper certified according to the standards of the FSC®.

MIA CASSANY
NATHALIE OUEDERNI

ANIMALS EVERYWHERE

ANIMAL HABITATS AROUND THE WORLD

LITTLE
GESTALTEN

EVERYTHING YOU CAN DISCOVER IN THIS BOOK

Dear reader,

In this book you will see some of the most amazing places on planet Earth. Each spot has been selected because it is home to thousands of spectacular animals and plants, so you are holding a real treasure in your hands! Discovering these wonderful places and learning about their important ecosystems is a real adventure for curious minds, so get ready to join us on a journey of discovery to these exciting places, learn their secrets, and get to know their creatures.

Have a good trip!

ARCTIC OCEAN

ARCTIC

ÉCRINS
NATIONAL PARK

DOÑANA
NATIONAL PARK

NORTH
AMERICA

GRAND
CANYON

PACIFIC
OCEAN

ATLANTIC
OCEAN

SAHARA
DESERT

SOUTH
AMERICA

AMAZON
RAINFOREST

IGUAZÚ FALLS

Ten key words for animal experts:

1. Gorge A narrow valley with steep walls created by a river.

2. Rainforest An ecosystem with a humid climate, lots of rain, and many different species. There are also **jungles,** which have much more dense vegetation on the forest floor as the tree canopy lets more light in.

3. Ocean A huge amount of salt water that covers large parts of Earth. There are five major oceans.

4. Mountain A high and often steep elevation in the land-scape. Many mountains together form a mountain range.

5. Beach A stretch of land along the coast that borders the sea, a river, or a lake. They are often sandy or stony.

6. Reef Like a city in the water, consisting of rocks and coral, where many different fish and other sea creatures live together.

7. Waterfall A flowing body of water that runs downhill over rocks into a pool below.

8. Wetland A water-rich landscape with many plants, where various birds live.

9. Island A land mass surrounded by water. Islands come in all sizes. A group of islands that lie close together and are often of volcanic origin is called an **archipelago.**

10. Desert An area where very few plants grow, either because it is very warm or because it is very cold. In dry deserts it is much colder at night than during the day.

PLACES TO DISCOVER

EUROPE

BLACK FOREST

MADDALENA ARCHIPELAGO

KAHUZI-BIEGA NATIONAL PARK

AFRICA

KILIMANJARO NATIONAL PARK

BOULDERS BEACH

ASIA

RED BEACH OF PANJIN

MOUNT FUJI

PACIFIC OCEAN

INDIAN OCEAN

On this map you can see each area of the world that can be explored in this book. You will also find a small globe on each double page, marking the area you are looking at so that you don't get lost on your journey!

AUSTRALIA

GREAT BARRIER REEF

ANTARCTIC OCEAN

ANTARCTIC

THE GRAND CANYON (USA)

In the north of the state of Arizona lies one of the most fascinating landscapes in the world: the Grand Canyon. Over many millions of years, the Colorado River (one of the longest rivers in North America) carved a huge gorge into the red rock, creating new and deeper waterways through the landscape, leading to the plateau growing and eventually drying out. Then something extraordinary happened—although a dry landscape had been created, many animals and plants found it provided an ideal habitat.

Coyote

Coyotes are very good hunters because they have excellent hearing and a fantastic sense of smell. They can even track down prey such as mice, snakes, and raccoons, which like to hide in underground caves or under blankets of snow in the Grand Canyon.

California condor

This spectacular animal is the largest flying bird in North America. It glides on air currents with outstretched wings and can even fly at altitudes of 15,000 feet (4,500 meters). A scavenger, it feeds on carrion (the remains of animals that it finds already dead). Sometimes it eats so much that it has to rest for several hours before it can fly again! For the Indigenous Navajo people, the California condor is a very special animal—they regard it as sacred.

Kaibab squirrel

These squirrels use their bushy tail in lots of different ways: to keep their balance when climbing, to keep them warm when it's cold, and to signal to other squirrels when danger is near.

Gray fox

This species of fox is the only one that can climb trees, thanks to its powerful claws. The gray fox is very intelligent and has excellent hearing, which enables it to locate even very quiet prey, making it a very good hunter.

KAHUZI-BIEGA NATIONAL PARK (DEMOCRATIC REPUBLIC OF CONGO)

Kahuzi-Biega is one of the globe's most important national parks, as its rainforests are home to some of the last eastern lowland gorillas in the world. Due to deforestation, fires and poaching in their natural habitats around the world, they are threatened with extinction. Fortunately, the park is now a protected area. As a result of this conservation work, it has once again become a safe home to these huge, social, intelligent primates. Gorillas also play an important role in the ecosystem, distributing the seeds of some of the plants that they eat, helping them to grow in different parts of the jungle.

Eastern lowland gorillas are among the largest primates in existence. Standing on their hind legs, males can grow up to 6.4 feet (1.96 meters) tall and weigh up to 441 pounds (200 kilograms). Females grow to a maximum height of 5 feet (1.5 meters) and weigh up to 216 pounds (98 kilograms).

Gorillas are diurnal animals (meaning that they are active during the daylight hours and sleep at night) and spend most of their mornings foraging for food before resting and then foraging again, eating as much as possible. At night they will build themselves a nest on the jungle floor, making a new one each time.

GORILLA MENU

✱ Gorillas eat an average of 40 pounds (18 kilograms) of plants per day, but could eat much more.

✱ Gorillas are herbivores, eating a vegetarian diet of around 104 different fruits.

✱ Gorillas hardly drink any water, getting almost all the liquid they need to survive from the plants they eat.

These gorillas have long fur that protects them from both high and low temperatures.

Unlike humans, their arms are longer than their legs. This is why they can climb and swing effortlessly between plants and vines and reach the highest branches of trees.

Although they are among the most intelligent animals and even use tools, gorillas cannot swim!

THE ARCTIC

The Arctic is one of the most remote regions on our planet. It stretches north across the Arctic Ocean and includes small parts of some of the coldest countries on Earth. Although it may not look like it, it is an area teeming with life—it is home to fish, birds, and millions of ice-dwelling organisms, and human communities such as the Inuit live in the far north. As nomadic people, they can follow the migrations of the animals they hunt, such as polar bears, seals, and walruses.

The region is also home to Arctic hares, Arctic foxes, Arctic wolves, orcas and musk oxen.

ANIMALS OF THE ARCTIC

Polar bear

In winter, polar bears live in complete darkness at temperatures as low as -85 degrees Fahrenheit (-65 degrees Celsius).

Caribou

The caribou's nose works like a heater, warming the air it breathes in.

Seal

Using their whiskers, seals are able to sense movement in the water and catch their prey or orient themselves while swimming in the ocean.

The Arctic ice acts like a refrigerator for the global climate. It reflects the sun's heat back into space, keeping the planet cool.

FRANKLIN EXPEDITION

The eternal ice can preserve stories, freezing them for hundreds of years and only later tell us what has long been forgotten. One of the most recent examples is the failed British voyage of the Franklin expedition: more than 170 years ago, while searching for new shipping routes between the East and West, two of the most advanced ships of their time disappeared without a trace. Witnesses speculated that they had been involved in an accident due to the dense fog. It was not until 2014 and 2016 that their wrecks were discovered north of Canada.

Inuit means "people" in their language, Inuktitut. *Inuk* is the singular and means "human" or "person."

KILIMANJARO NATIONAL PARK (TANZANIA)

Kilimanjaro is the highest mountain in Africa. The dormant volcano is located in Tanzania and its summit is covered in snow. In recent years, however, the snow on this breathtaking mountain has been melting and the region's ecosystem has been changing. Each of the five different ecological climate zones (the rainforest, the cultivation zone, the heather and moorland zone, the alpine desert zone, and the Arctic zone) are important for preserving biodiversity and protecting animal and plant life.

Family first

Elephants are herd animals, which means they live together in groups. Each herd is led by a dominant elephant cow (a female). Within the herd, the animals work together and protect each other.

Huge ears

Elephants have very large, powerful ears—do you know what they use them for? As fans! When it's hot, elephants flap their ears to cool themselves down, as if they have their own air-conditioning system!

A wildebeest survival strategy

Wildebeest have to watch out for predators. When they come to a river during their migration, for example, they face a major challenge. Crocodiles are waiting for them in the water and lions often get into position on the opposite bank. So the wildebeest work together: a few make a start and suddenly the whole herd jumps into the water at once. This surprises the predators, but some of the wildebeest are usually caught anyway.

Flying high!

Giraffes have very long necks, making them the tallest animals on Earth! With these long necks and very long, purple tongues they can reach the highest leaves to eat them. Giraffes have to use its neck muscles to move their heads downwards.

Unique spots

Each giraffe has a uniquely patterned coat, comparable to human fingerprints. They have more sweat glands on the spots than on the lighter parts, the skin is thicker and the area underneath is particularly well supplied with blood so that it doesn't get too hot.

Drinking in groups

Wildebeest are known for their great migration between the Serengeti National Park in Tanzania and the Masai Mara National Reserve in Kenya. In a natural spectacle, millions of the animals travel hundreds of miles to find grass and fresh water. Once there, they drink a lot, doing so in groups to protect themselves.

A big heart

Giraffes have very large hearts—they can grow as big as a watermelon! They need these huge hearts to pump blood through their long necks and into their heads. This is how they ensure every part of their body is adequately supplied with oxygen.

BOULDERS BEACH (SOUTH AFRICA)

At the southern tip of Africa, where the Atlantic and Indian oceans meet, lies Boulders Beach, near Cape Town. It is known for its colony of African penguins, which live there all year round. African penguins are an endangered species, so it is important to protect and care for them.

In the wild, penguins can live up to 20 years.

African penguins may look clumsy and sometimes a bit funny, but they are actually very fast and agile swimmers. They can swim at speeds of up to 20 miles per hour (32 kilometers per hour).

Due to habitat loss, overfishing and pollution, African penguins are threatened with extinction. Species conservation is important for their survival.

African penguins are monogamous birds, mating with one partner for their entire lives.

These penguins are recognizable by the striking feather pattern of a black and white horseshoe shape/semicircle around their eyes.

They are very social animals. Together with many others of their species, they form breeding colonies to protect and care for their young.

Although they are aquatic animals, African penguins can also walk on land, although they feel most comfortable in the water.

There are 18 species of penguins around the world, but these are the only kind that live on the coast of Africa.

MOUNT FUJI (JAPAN)

Mount Fuji is a volcano in Japan and the highest mountain in the country. The weather conditions at its high altitudes are extreme. However, there are some animals that have managed to adapt and live in this region.

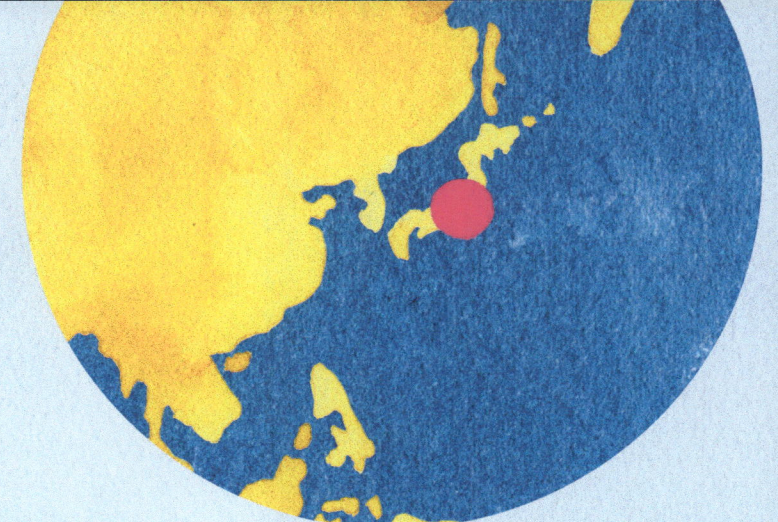

ANIMALS AROUND MOUNT FUJI

Japanese fox

The fox lives in various areas of Japan, including in the forests and on the slopes of Mount Fuji, and plays a special role in Japanese culture.

Sika deer

This deer species is native to East Asia, likes to be near bodies of water, and lives in the forest region around Mount Fuji. They are good swimmers, so are able flee from predators into rivers or lakes.

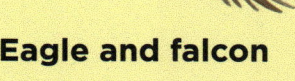

Eagle and falcon

Birds of prey, like eagles and falcons, hunt at higher altitudes on the mountain. In Japan, dreaming of Mount Fuji, a falcon, and an eggplant at the start of the new year is said to bring good luck.

THE FOX IN JAPANESE MYTHOLOGY

Kitsune

In Japanese mythology, foxes are mythical creatures called *kitsune.* It is believed that *kitsune* have magical powers, can change shape, and even take on human form.

Magical tail

According to legend, the number of tails a *kitsune* has indicates his age and wisdom: the older he gets, the more tails he grows and the more powerful he becomes. In some stories *kitsune* have have up to nine tails.

Temple guardian

At sacred sites, *kitsune* are believed to have a protective role. Therefore fox statues are sometimes placed at the entrances to temples.

GET TO KNOW SIKA DEER A LITTLE BETTER

Where do they live?

Originally from East Asia, sika deer were later brought to other parts of the world, such as Europe and North America.

Coat

Sika deer have different coat colors, ranging from reddish-brown to gray. The coloration is usually related to the environment they live in so that they can camouflage themselves better.

Specific vocalizations

In addition to the usual sounds that deer make, sika deer produce a high-pitched whistle and other special sounds to communicate with members of their group.

THE GREAT BARRIER REEF (AUSTRALIA)

The Great Barrier Reef is the largest coral reef in the world. It is more than 1,243 miles (2,000 kilometers) long. Corals are not plants, rather they are cnidarians (like jellyfish). They consist of many small animals called polyps, which make colonies. If you look at the Great Barrier Reef in its entirety, you could say it is the largest creature in the world. The reef was formed over a hundred thousand years through the accumulation of countless coral skeletons. The algae that settle on the corals cause them to glow in lots of different colors. Coral reefs tend to develop just below sea level as they need sunlight to grow.

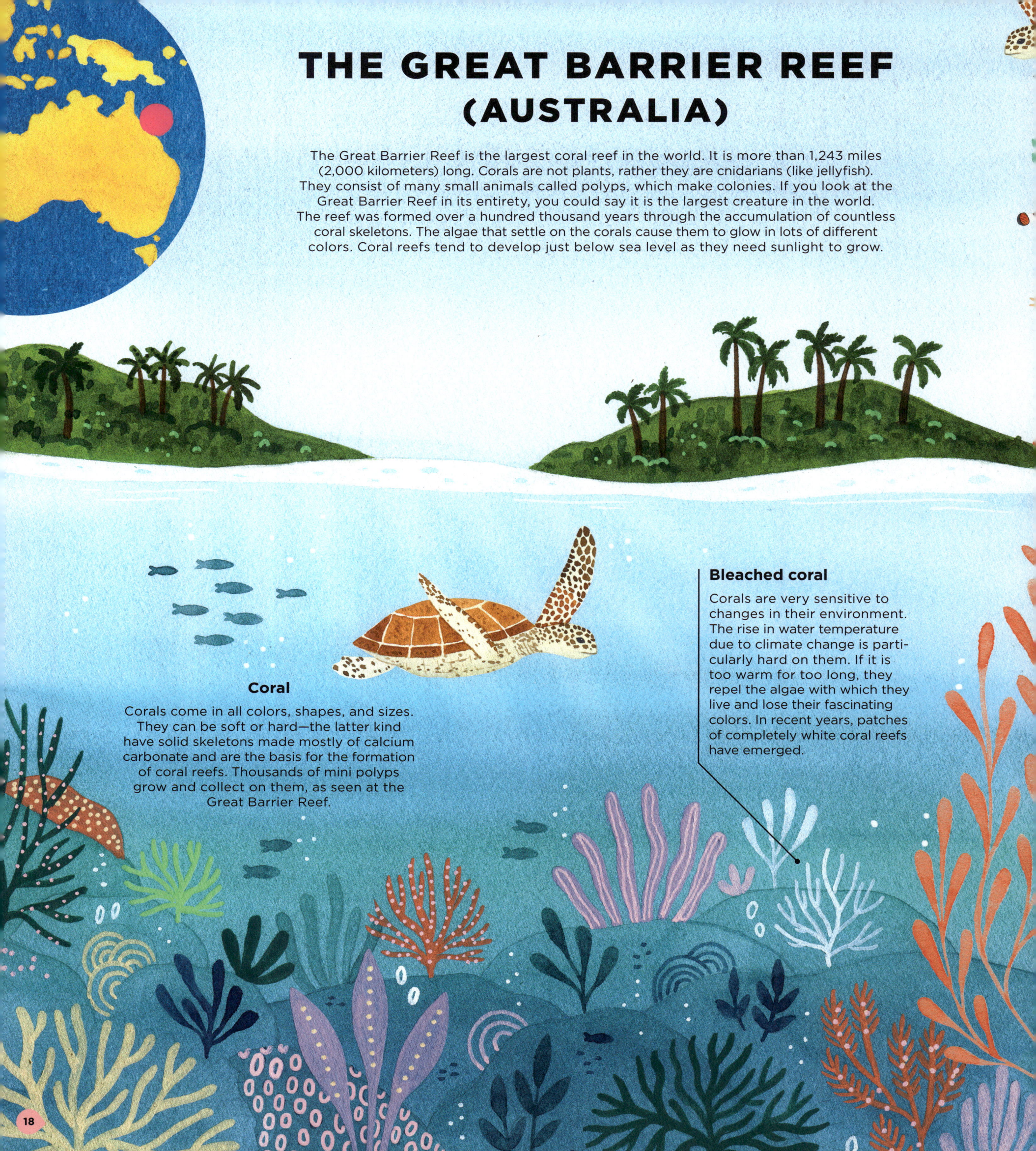

Coral

Corals come in all colors, shapes, and sizes. They can be soft or hard—the latter kind have solid skeletons made mostly of calcium carbonate and are the basis for the formation of coral reefs. Thousands of mini polyps grow and collect on them, as seen at the Great Barrier Reef.

Bleached coral

Corals are very sensitive to changes in their environment. The rise in water temperature due to climate change is particularly hard on them. If it is too warm for too long, they repel the algae with which they live and lose their fascinating colors. In recent years, patches of completely white coral reefs have emerged.

WHAT A COINCIDENCE!

The story goes that Captain James Cook was the first European to discover the Great Barrier Reef in 1770 when he ran aground on the reef with his ship *Endeavour*. Of course, the Indigenous people of Australia knew about the reef long before he did. Searching for a way out, the crew of the *Endeavour* explored the fascinating underwater world and then stripped their ship of goods and weapons to lighten its load, allowing them to enter an estuary and continue on their journey.

OTHER REEF DWELLERS

Seahorse

The female seahorse gives birth to the eggs and lays them in the male's abdominal pouch. The male incubates the eggs until baby seahorses hatch.

Clownfish

Clownfish live near or even inside anemones. Fortunately, they are immune to the stinging venom of anemone tentacles, so once they have found one they are protected from predators. The clownfish eat food left behind on the anemone and keep it clean. This is how they help each other!

Blue surgeonfish

Although they are normally harmless, these fish can sting! They have sharp spines at the base of their tails called scalpels.

Sea turtle

The ears of sea turtles are on the inside of their heads, which is why they have muffled hearing. Their beaks are particularly well suited to eating crabs, jellyfish, and other aquatic animals. Although they have no vocal chords they can still make sounds and communicate.

Starfish

If a starfish loses an arm, it grows back again, much like with crabs or lobsters.

THE RED BEACH OF PANJIN (CHINA)

The Red Beach of Panjin is known for its peculiar color. Every fall, a foxtail plant, the beach sod, turns the beach and its marshes a bright red. In order to preserve the incredible biodiversity of the landscape, the beach was declared a national nature reserve a long time ago. More than 260 bird species live here, making it a popular bird-watching destination.

Bird migration is a fascinating and complex phenomenon. Birds use various signals, like Earth's magnetic field and the stars, to find their way on their long-distance flights. They also have an incredible sense of orientation and memory, which enable them to find their way back to their wintering and breeding grounds year after year.

Bird migration begins in spring, when the birds leave the places where they have spent the winter. They arrive on the beach tired and weak, but they know this is a great place to feed, rest, and breed.

Manchurian cranes are particularly prized in East Asia for their beauty, flight patterns, and elegance. They are an endangered bird species and a popular symbol in many works of art in China.

Gray heron

The gray heron has a long neck and long legs. It feeds mainly on fish and crustaceans and can be found year round on the Red Beach of Panjin.

Osprey

This bird of prey appears on Panjin's Red Beach in spring and summer. It feeds mainly on fish, which it can find plenty of here, and leaves with a full belly.

Eurasian oystercatcher

The oystercatcher has a long orange beak to help it catch its food. Feeding mainly on mollusks and crustaceans, it not only has to catch them, but it also needs to know how to get to their meat.

Manchurian crane

Manchurian cranes are resident birds, which means they stay in one region and do not migrate. With its large expanses of water and dense reeds, this beach is an important breeding ground for these cranes.

IGUAZÚ FALLS (ARGENTINA AND BRAZIL)

The spectacular Iguazú Falls are part of the Iguazu River, in the border region between Argentina, Brazil, and Paraguay. In the language of the Guarani, an Indigenous population group in South America, Iguazú means "big water." This natural wonder was caused by a huge volcanic eruption thousands of years ago. The falls are considered one of the seven natural wonders of the world and are a Unesco World Heritage site. They consist of 275 waterfalls, including Garganta del Diablo, the highest of them all, which has a drop of 269 feet (82 meters).

This fascinating and unique water world is home to hundreds of bird species, many mammal species, and a large variety of insects.

The Iguazú National Park is home to endangered animals such as the tapir and anteater. Both have beautiful and distinctive noses and a preference for solitude. While the anteater can sleep up to 15 hours a day, the tapir devotes itself to scattering the seeds of the fruits it eats via its droppings. They are also known as "gardeners," as this is how they spread the plants in the surrounding area.

The Devil's Throat

Garganta del Diablo translates as Devil's Throat—a fitting name, as according to Guarani legend, an angry snake god created this waterfall after his betrothed had fled with another man in a canoe. Out of anger, he cut a gorge in the river, the Devil's Mouth, and turned the girl into a rock and her lover into a tree.

The sooty swift

This bird is native to the region and is considered a symbol of the Iguazú Falls. It is the only animal that builds its nest behind the falls. To do so, it flies through the falling water to the other side.

Nighttime rainbows

On some nights, the full moon casts its light through the steam of the Iguazú Falls and you can see beautiful rainbows—even in the middle of the night! Combined with the surrounding nocturnal sounds and the roar of the water-falls, seeing one is said by locals to be an unforgettable experience.

Other animal inhabitants

Turtles and herons also live around the Iguazú Falls. Both species are sensitive animals. It is important to protect the area so that they can continue to live here.

THE AMAZON RAINFOREST (SOUTH AMERICA)

The world's largest tropical rainforest grows in the basin of the Amazon, one of the longest rivers in the world. With an area of more than 2.3 million square miles (6 million square kilometers), it is larger than India and stretches across nine countries (Brazil, Peru, Venezuela, Colombia, Bolivia, Ecuador, Suriname, Guyana, and French Guiana). The Amazon rainforest is the most biodiverse area in the world: around 10 percent of all known animal and plant species on Earth live here. Despite the deforestation that threatens this region, there are still more than 350 billion trees in the Amazon rainforest. In the midst of this dense and lush vegetation live some Indigenous tribes. This is a truly fabulous part of the world.

THE LUNGS OF THE PLANET

It is said that the rainforest functions like our lungs. It balances oxygen (O_2) and carbon (CO_2) in the air. Plants and trees produce oxygen, which we need to breathe. When human beings breathe out, we exhale carbon dioxide (CO_2), which plants and trees need to live. To protect our environment they must remain balanced. CO_2 is also emitted by industry, and as a result there is too much of it in the air, which can lead to global warming. It is therefore particularly important to protect the rainforest, which produces incredible amounts of oxygen.

Indigenous Tribes

It may seem unbelievable, but there are still some ethnic groups in this jungle who live largely without contact with the outside world. Many of these tribes have opted for a mixture of traditional and modern ways of life.

The Amazon

Originally, individual sections of the river were given different names by the Indigenous tribes living alongside it. Then, Europeans gave a lot of places their own names, leading to many Indigenous names being forgotten in large parts of the world.

SOME FASCINATING INHABITANTS

Green anaconda

This anaconda is one of the largest snakes in existence: it is, on average, 6.6 to 16.4 feet (2 to 5 meters) long, and particularly heavy specimens weigh over 176.3 pounds (80 kilograms).

Electric Eel

These creatures live in the mud of the riverbed and can generate electric shocks of up to 860 volts—to compare, 120 volts come out of the sockets in your home!

Capybara

The largest and most sociable rodent in the world resembles a guinea pig and is also a peaceful inhabitant of the Amazon rainforest.

Poison dart frog

Although these frogs are tiny and look harmless with their beautiful colors, they are so poisonous that some Indigenous tribes smear their arrows with the secretions from their skin to make them more effective when hunting.

Jaguar

Jaguars are excellent hunters because they have the strongest jaw muscles in the cat world. But they are also excellent swimmers and divers. They spend a lot of time in the water to cool off, move around, and hunt.

Brown-mantled Tamarin

The brown-mantled tamarin was first sighted in 2007 and cataloged by scientists in 2009—an incredible recent discovery! There is evidence that there is still an enormous number of undiscovered species in the Amazon rainforest.

DOÑANA NATIONAL PARK (SPAIN)

The Doñana National Park is a biosphere reserve—a place where great importance is attached to preserving biodiversity. It is home to many unique animal and plant species and is therefore particularly worthy of protection. But it is struggling with drought, so a lot has to be done to protect everything that lives there.

Shifting sand dunes

The sand that makes up the dunes is constantly in motion due to the wind, causing them to change shape. The dunes move about 10–20 feet (3–6 meters) per year.

Among the most famous inhabitants of the area are pink flamingos. These large and beautiful birds gather in the marshes of Doñana to feed and raise their young.

The region is a true paradise for migratory birds that return here every year. Millions come to Doñana National Park from different parts of Europe and Africa to rest, feed, and mate.

THE ANIMALS OF DOÑANA

Doñana National Park is not only home to birds, italso provides the perfect habitat for many other animals.

Iberian lynx

With its spotted coat, the Iberian lynx is one of the rarest cats in the world. It is a very good hunter, but unfortunately threatened with extinction.

Deer

Deer are particularly active animals. They can run very fast and jump very high.

Fox

The fox used to feed on wild rabbits, but due to a decline in their numbers now eats carrion, birds, and small mammals.

THE BLACK FOREST (GERMANY)

Dense forests as far as the eye can see and trees in the most varied shades of green characterize this region. The Black Forest is a fascinating mountain range in the southwest of Germany. It rains much more here than in other German regions. This is why trees and plants grow particularly well in this part of the world, as plants need a lot of moisture to grow. What is astonishing about this place is that the temperatures do not fluctuate very much at high altitudes. However, there are often very strong winds and, of course snow, especially in winter.

Fern

Ferns bear neither flowers nor fruit, and when they grow, all their fronds unfurl from tightly coiled snail shapes at the center of the plants. Ferns have been around so long that they have been found as fossils.

Foxglove

Foxglove is a valuable plant, as it can be used for medicinal purposes. But be careful—it is very poisonous and dangerous to eat!

Spruce

This conifer has very dense branches. Some people say that the Black Forest gets its name from these trees. With their dark green needles, which make it difficult for the sun to shine through, they make the forest a dark but protected place.

UNIQUE ANIMALS OF THE REGION

Hinterwald cow

These are a very old breed of cattle. They are small and agile, which is why they can live particularly well in this region. Cows are ruminants (grazing animals), which means that they get the most out of their food by chewing it several times.

Black Forest Coldblood horse

This is the name of a special breed of horse that was originally bred for heavy forest work in the region. They are very robust and hardy and have a brown coat and a beautiful light-colored mane and tail.

THE MADDALENA ARCHIPELAGO (SARDINIA)

The Maddalena archipelago consists of more than 60 islands of different sizes, all with beautiful landscapes. Some of them are even uninhabited, so there is a natural diversity of plants and animals. The sea around the archipelago is known for its incredible clarity, making it look turquoise. To keep it that way, we need to protect the water.

Dolphin

Bottlenose dolphins and common dolphins are two of the most beautiful and entertaining inhabitants of this region. These calm animals can often be seen swimming in large groups, making huge leaps and twirling through the air.

Sea turtle

The waters of the archipelago are also home to loggerhead turtles and green sea turtles. In the sea around the islands, they feed on small crustaceans like crabs, or mollusks, jellyfish, or underwater plants such as seagrass.

ARCHIPELAGO

An archipelago is a group of islands that lie close to each other and are surrounded by sea or ocean. Indonesia is the largest archipelago state in the world, with over 17,000 islands.

Seabird

The archipelago is also an important site for various seabird species. The gull, cormorant, and Cory's shearwater live here. It is an ideal refuge for them to breed and rest during their migrations.

Monk seal

Although monk seals are threatened with extinction, the Maddalena archipelago is one of the few places where they can still be found. Monk seals live together in small colonies of around 20 animals.

THE SAHARA DESERT (NORTH AFRICA)

Welcome to the largest of the world's hot deserts! Deserts are areas on our planet where it rains very, very rarely. Due to the lack of water, there are few creatures that can survive in these places. Some of the animals that can tend to hide under the sand all day long, only coming out a night to hunt and feed. Here are three of the most spectacular animals that can withstand the extreme conditions of the Sahara.

Mendes antelope

This antelope is undoubtedly remarkable for its beautiful horns, which grow upwards in a spiral and wave-like pattern. Mendes antelopes do not need to drink, as they get the liquid they need from their food. They move in small groups of around 20 animals in search of shrubs and grasses to graze on. Unfortunately, they are threatened with extinction and only live in a few areas of Africa today.

Dromedary

Dromedaries are a type of camel, but they only have one hump. Nomadic peoples keep them as pack animals to transport their belongings. They are well built for this due to their amazing speed and stamina. They are able to withstand extreme heat and cold, and can close their nostrils completely to protect themselves from dust and sand.

Naqab desert scorpion

This small animal, about 4 inches (10 centimeters) long, has a thin yellow tail that ends with a dangerous venomous stinger, which can deliver a life-threatening and very, very painful sting for us humans. In the desert, this scorpion hides in all kinds of crevices or under stones.

ÉCRINS NATIONAL PARK (FRANCE)

This national park in the French Alps is known for its high mountains and the varied animal and plant life that make it their home. Many different animal species live on its high peaks and glaciers, in the forests and valleys, and in the rivers, lakes, and meadows. The park is also home to one of the highest mountains in France, the Barre des Écrins, and the freshwater mountain lakes are teeming with life.

HOW IS A GLACIER FORMED?

For glaciers to form, it has to be very cold in one place for a very long time—so cold that the fallen snow does not melt. It is coldest on high mountains. If it has snowed heavily in winter and they are covered with snow, the snow begins to accumulate on the summit and becomes denser and heavier over time. Because of its weight, the lower snow turns into ice. This ice slides down into the valleys due to gravity, as if it were a very slow-moving river. As it does, it takes rocks, soil, and other materials with it, cleaning the mountain floor in the process.

Glaciers are very important for our planet because they store large amounts of water in the form of ice. When the ice melts, the water flows out and fills rivers and lakes, making them essentially large reservoirs. Glaciers also shape the mountain landscape: when they move, they cut deep valleys into the earth below them.

This process is not only beautiful to look at, but also extremely important for the well-being of the planet and its ecosystems. Unfortunately, global warming is causing temperatures to rise so much that the millennia-old ice on the glaciers is melting, putting the habitats of animals, plants, and humans in danger.

SOME ANIMALS OF THIS REGION

Kingfisher

This colorful bird is a skilled angler and can often be found near the rivers and lakes of the national park. It's recognizable by its bright blue feathers and long, pointed beak.

Otter

The European otter is also an inhabitant of these mountains. It is an aquatic mammal, living in rivers and lakes.

Grass frog

The upper side of the grass frog can be yellowish, reddish, or dark brown in color. It goes hunting for insects at night, but during the day it prefers to hide in damp places.

Alpine newt

The alpine newt is an amphibian that lives near the lakes and ponds of the national park. It can be recognized by its spotted skin and unique, four-toed feet.

IN THE AIR

IN THE WATER

FLAMINGO

Five facts:

✳ The pink color of these birds is due to their diet, which is rich in algae and crustaceans whose pigments dye their feathers.

✳ With their curved necks and long legs, flamingos are instantly recognizable. Like most things in the animal world, their appearance has a purpose: the long, slender legs allow them to walk in shallow water, and thanks to their long necks they are able to feed on shellfish and plants below the surface.

✳ When they have to fly for many miles, they form a V in the air like many other birds. This means they use less energy because they meet less headwind.

✳ Flamingos are famous for their mating dances.

✳ They make sounds that resemble caws, whistles, and squeaks.

DOLPHIN

Five facts:

✳ Dolphins have the ability to echolocate. This means that they send out sound waves and then work out where their echo is coming from. This is how they orient themselves and locate their prey.

✳ Dolphin groups are called pods and can contain as many as 100 members. They work together to find food, protect, and care for each other.

✳ Dolphins love to play and have fun in many different ways: they jump and pirouette or throw seaweed to each other as if it were a ball.

✳ Dolphins communicate through many different sounds, which sometimes seem like whistles or clicking noises to us.

✳ Dolphins are among the most intelligent animals in the world. They recognize and call each other, for example by whistling different names.

FASCINATING FACTS

A QUESTION OF CLOTHING

SHELL

The shell of a turtle consists of solid bone plates. It is part of its skeleton and grows with it. The back shell and belly shell are connected by a cartilage bridge. Turtles can feel when you touch their shell as it presses on the membranous tissue that lies beneath it.

FEATHERS

Feathers are true jacks-of-all-trades. They are mostly used for flying, which is why they are streamlined, allowing birds to fly smoothly and quietly. Birds also use their feathers to protect themselves from the cold or to attract attention with their bright colors during the mating season.

SKIN

A snake's skin is covered with scales, which are waterproof and quite hard. As a snake grows, its skin cannot expand as much as its body, so the snake has to shed and renew it.

THE COLOR OF FUR

The fact that most animals in cold, snowy, and icy landscapes are white is no coincidence. This color serves as camouflage in the snow so that they cannot be seen by predators, or so that they themselves are not seen when hunting their prey. Depending on the environment, animals can develop very different coat colors and patterns.

ANTLERS AND HORNS

Horns and antlers vary greatly, depending on the species. Animals like deer shed and renew their antlers each year, while horns usually continue to grow throughout an animal's life (as seen with the Mendes antelope).

THE STRONGEST HUNTERS

ORCA

Five facts:

✻ Orcas have sharp teeth and are among the fastest predators in the sea. They can swim up to 35 miles per hour (56 kilometers per hour)!

✻ Orcas are very intelligent. They can communicate, learn, adapt to different needs, and pass on what they have learned to their descendants.

✻ Orcas live in strong family groups called pods. The females and their offspring form the core of the community.

✻ Orcas hunt as teams, communicating and using different strategies. For example, some of them surround their prey while the others attack the prey from below.

✻ As they hunt as teams, orcas also share their prey.

EAGLE

Five facts:

✻ Eagles have exceptional eyesight, which is much sharper than that of humans. This enables them to see their prey from a great distance.

✻ They usually fly elegantly and majestically through the air and suddenly drop into a dive to hunt. Their prey is thus taken by surprise and often has no time to get to safety.

✻ Eagles grab their prey while in the air using their talons. Other large birds of prey, like the osprey, can grab floating food from under the surface of water as it flies by, holding on to it even when the prey is heavy and wriggly.

✻ Their curved beaks are very strong. They can easily tear off the flesh of their prey using them.

✻ Eagles can fly up to 15,000 feet (4570 meters) high.

FASCINATING FACTS

A QUESTION OF SIZE!

THE BIG ONES

Gorillas are the largest primates on Earth. On average, a male silverback weighs around 418 pounds (190 kilograms) and measures around 5.5 feet (1.6 meters) when upright. The span of their outstretched arms can be as much as 8 feet (2.5 meters).

The **African bush elephant** (also called African savanna elephant) is the heaviest land animal, weighing up to 22,000 pounds (10,000 kilograms).

Measured from their hooves to their ossiciones (the skin-covered bone structures at the top of their heads), the tallest mammals on land are **giraffes.** They can grow up to 20 feet (6 meters) tall. They are herbivores rather than predators, preferring to eat the lush green leaves found on the treetops.

THE LITTLE ONES

The smallest **scorpion** is the *Microbuthus pusillus* from the Buthidae family, measuring just 0.25 inches (6.5 millimeters).

Some **seahorses** are only 0.5 to 1.05 inches (1.5 to 2.5 centimeters) in size and extremely light, although their exact weight is unknown.

Among the most dangerous frogs in the world are **poison dart frogs** (also called poison frogs or poison arrow frogs), even though they are only between 0.5 and 2.5 inches (1.5 and 6 centimeters) in size.

Capybara

Although they come from the guinea pig family, capybara are quite large, growing to a height of around 25 inches (63 centimeters). They are peaceful and feel protected in larger groups of their own kind. Their natural enemies are mainly predatory cats such as the jaguar or the ocelot. Thanks to their relaxed and sociable nature, they have many friends among animal species—they don't even have to be afraid of crocodiles.

To Gaia, our Earth, and to all
the creatures that inhabit it.
Nathalie

TO S.B.,
for being my natural
habitat on this planet.
Mia